Making the Pennies Drop

Gail Hugman

MAKING THE PENNIES DROP

© 2024 Gail Hugman. All rights reserved.

Paperback ISBN: 978-1-7384757-0-4
Ebook ISBN: 978-1-7384757-1-1

The right of Gail Hugman to be identified as the author of this work has been asserted by them in accordance with the Copyright, Designs and Patents Act 1988. All rights reserved, no part of this publication may be reproduced, stored in, or introduced into a retrieval system, or transmitted, in any form, or by any means (electronic, mechanical, photocopying, recording, or otherwise) without the prior written permission of the publisher. Any person who does any unauthorised act in relation to this publication may be liable to criminal prosecution and civil claims for damages.

Book design by Sarah E. Holroyd (https://sleepingcatbooks.com)

In memory of my mother, Tess, who gave each of us a list of little jobs each day and, as we did them, she took the time to do the all-important tick I loved so much! Such is the ingenuity of mothers.

Contents

Disclaimer	vii
'Why should I?'	1
'You can't make me!'	6
Best Results Come When You Remember These Points	12
The birth of a baby is the birth of a brain!	17
Deciding where to start	21
The Timeline	25
How life events can affect children's learning	34
Assessment Activity 1: Juggling	39
Assessment Activity 2: Random Shapes – A 3-Minute Memory Challenge	45
Assessment Activity 3: Memory – Known Objects	48
Assessment Activity 4: Short-Term Memory – Listening	51
Identifying your child's core needs by interpreting their behaviour	55
Self-Control	62
Activity 1: Grandmother's footsteps	64
Activity 2: The Voice Game	64
Activity 3: 10 Steps and Change	65
Activity 4: Brain Challenge	65
Focus and Attention	75
Activity 1: The Balance Skill	77
Activity 2: The Water Challenge	77

Activity 3: Advanced Water Challenge	78
Time Management	80
Activity: One-minute exercises	82
Planning	87
Organisation	91
Exercise 1: Sorting	92
Exercise 2: Organisation	94
Exercise 3: Colouring	95
Working Memory	97
Activity 1: Brain Train – Memory	98
Activity 2: Brain Train – Pictures for Memory	99
Activity 3: The Shop Game	101
Activity 4: Alphabetical Shop Game	102
'Oh! Now I get it!'	104
And finally…a reminder	107
Just one more thing…	108

Disclaimer

Although the author has made every effort to ensure that the information in this book was correct at press time and while this publication is designed to provide accurate information in regard to the subject matter covered, the author assumes no responsibility for errors, inaccuracies, omissions, or any other inconsistencies herein and hereby disclaims any liability to any party for any loss, damage, or disruption caused by errors or omissions, whether such errors or omissions result from negligence, accident, or any other cause.

Any case studies used are a composite of families or children that the author has worked with over fifty years, and do not represent any individual.

Branded games named in this publication are resources the author has personally used and found effective. The author has no affiliation with any company, nor any incentive for naming particular retail games.

This publication is meant as a source of valuable information for the reader; however, it is not meant as a substitute for direct expert assistance. If such level of assistance is required, the services of a competent professional should be sought.

'Why should I?'

This, of all questions, must be the one that defeats even the most resilient of parents – and teachers – at times! Certainly, even very young children learn quickly to 'push your buttons' and can drive you to the depths of despair at times. As one mother once cried, having slammed the door so hard it broke one of its hinges, 'I used to run six countries and I'm being controlled by a six-year-old! What is *wrong* with me?'

Take a breath...there is absolutely nothing wrong with you.

You are the best parent there could ever possibly be for your child. The reason you – and your child – get so frustrated is because you're pulling in different directions.

Your child is doing 'what comes naturally'; you're trying to teach them to behave properly and do well in life when you yourself have little or no guidance, other than your own upbringing and everyone else's opinions.

Take another breath...this book is going to give you a different way to look at things and, hopefully, an easier way forward.

You, as a parent, are perfect for the job – you need to know this so that your self-belief encourages your child to believe in your guidance and leadership. And now, more than ever in this contradictory world, your child needs you.

To begin...

Have you ever stopped to look at *how much* has changed since you were a child? Not only our use of technology (did your classmates have mobile phones? iPad?), but also our expectations, diet, working habits, and environment.

Thinking about it, we must also include the pressures on society in general, added by the ever-increasing population: levels of anxiety (which has increased since the pandemic), across all socio-economic groups, cost-of-living crises, environmental extremism, hostilities, and migration around the globe.

Today's world is different in so many ways from the one you grew up in; there are more challenges to consider – and it feels as though there is less time to just 'be'. Many parents share anxieties about this.

You also share anxieties about your child's education. Should they learn a musical instrument – especially if they won't practise? What should you do if they don't like reading? What happens if they don't have a mobile phone, like 'all their friends'? How much screen time is *safe*? Should you read with them every day? What about discipline, and what exactly *are* consequences?

These worries crop up throughout the primary years and beyond, and so parents often find themselves in a position where they need to think on their weary feet.

Periodically, against your better nature, you resort to cajoling, pleading, 'because I said so', and even bribery to get things done, and then feel disappointed with yourself as if you're somehow letting down your child.

When it comes to helping your children, there are things you *feel* you should know (but kind of don't really, which is not your fault) and there are things that you are told you should do, but there's also too much conflicting information that can be mind boggling.

This book aims to explain the reasoning behind what your child needs to learn so that *your* confidence grows because you'll know what your child is developing, what you can do about it at home, and why.

There are also things children get confused about at school and in life, but they haven't got the verbal skills to explain, or don't know who to ask. It can start to make everything seem so complicated to them, so they shut down.

This book is intended to work for *both* parents and children:

- Parents can read it by themselves and then dip in and out, working on it with their child.

AND

- The magic can start to happen when parent and child work together on this book as a team.

This book aims to help support you so you feel more confident about your child's learning, and you can pass that confidence on to them, so you help them grow to reach their potential as well-rounded human beings who know what they want in life.

The book is full of insights and information, drawn from my fifty years of teaching experience, that work to help satisfy your child's natural drive to learn and become independent and successful in a difficult world.

You will find easy-to-use assessment tools and the way to interpret your child's performance, and then what to do to make progress. A range of activities, along with the instructions that make them effective, are also included. They are not one-off activities – variations are given, so you can use them repeatedly, until you feel your child is confident with the skill they are aiming to achieve.

'You can't make me!'

These words, and others like them such as, 'I hate you!', 'No!', 'won't', and 'can't', may be where you're starting from. If it is, don't panic; take a slight shift in approach.

Although these words have the power to induce fury and indignation in even the most patient of us, in the heat of the moment, you may say something you'll regret – because you don't *really* want to take away the play station, or stop them going on the school trip, or ban TV for a week – because you know deep down it's not *actually* going to solve anything.

If a situation has escalated to this point, there is only one action you can safely take, and that is to stop.

Remember, your child is reacting (unconsciously) to a feeling – and it isn't a positive feeling.

You, however, have developed the ability to consciously *respond to* what you're feeling. You have more choice than they do because they have not yet developed that level of self-control.

Yes, you may be seething because of the way they've spoken to you. Yes, you feel like you want to yell and slam doors. But don't. Resist the urge to storm off or bang doors. Above all, don't ignore. Just stop.

Give yourself time to think.

Give your brain fresh oxygen with a nice deep breath.

Regain your own balance.

Let your instinct come into play. The actions and activities in this book have been used successfully with neurodiverse children as well as neurotypical children. If you suspect your child is neurodiverse, speak to their school and your G.P. to arrange an assessment. Further specialised assistance may be needed from a psychologist or specialist teacher.

This is a child you care more about than anyone, and they are obviously struggling. Who else can they yell at? You're their safety valve.

Whatever triggered the behaviour, they know they shouldn't talk to you that way, but now isn't the time to remind them.

Let them know you're sorry they feel the need to react like this and you don't really understand why. Tell them that when they've calmed themselves down, you'll be ready to listen to what their problem is and help them work out how to solve it, because no one is feeling happy right now. Whether they are neurotypical or neurodiverse, you may need to help them by quietly talking them through calming techniques.

This will give you a starting point.

It's a big ask, I know, but they need your leadership. They need to feel they can talk to you without fear of judgement or 'lecturing'.

It isn't necessarily a reflection of your parenting skills; it isn't necessarily anything to do with you personally at all. It is to do with the conflict we all face at some point between what we intuitively feel and know to be 'right', and the contradictions we meet in life, including the pressure to work at speeds that are uncomfortable for us at times. The important thing now is that you create the space for communication with your child, human to human.

Real Life Example 1
At 15, Thomas was meant to be studying for GCSEs, but he wasn't, and he wouldn't. It was already March, with exams looming in May, and Mum was at her wit's end. No amount of pleading, nagging, cajoling, or explaining had helped. It had reached stalemate.

The greatest fear of any child is that you will be disappointed with them because they have let you down in some way. In their (subconscious) mind, it is better to keep quiet than blurt out that they can't cope.

So, you need to find out what has led them to this point.

When everyone had calmed down and agreed to listen, Thomas said he didn't understand *how* to study for exams. Why should he? He hadn't been shown.

He, too, was deeply worried because he wasn't sure who to ask for help. He was being told by his teachers to revise but didn't know what 'revise' looked like. He had printed notes from teachers on each subject, but wasn't sure how the notes related to his course work; were they 'extra', 'instead of', or something else? Added to this, it had never occurred to Thomas that *he* should plan his time; nobody had ever suggested it or shown him how.

In short, Thomas was completely overwhelmed and not only *felt* he was going to fail but was being *told* he was going to fail if he didn't 'get on with it'. So, he shut down.

It took just three teaching sessions to get Thomas on track.

He was keen to succeed; he just needed to know how.

One session was on planning his revision and how to approach it, one session was on organising his time and resources, and one session looked at the bigger picture – what he was hoping to achieve and how to get there. This all led him to pass all his exams with good grades, just a couple of hardworking months later.

Real Life Example 2

Sasha's busy, professional working mum told me, 'My 5-year-old has everything she could wish for in her room. She has all the best toys, games, TV, everything. But she sits and screams at me under the table when I try to take her swimming.'

One simple action solved this: breakfast with Mum once a week, to the exclusion of all else. No siblings. No phone. No distractions. Mum's total attention to listen, to encourage, and to let Sasha know that Mum had *chosen* to spend time with her was all it took for her behaviour to transform.

If the promise is kept because your child sees it is important to you as well, they will feel they matter and will look forward to their 1-2-1 time with you, because it is special to them.

We can avoid many of the difficulties that lead to children being overloaded by paying attention to apparently minor details, like the time we give, and being very careful what we assume they know, think, or can do. It is always better to check; this is reassuring for your child's confidence and self-esteem.

You will see from this book how important it is for children to receive feedback and recognition. They will patiently wait for it. They don't mind if it is only once a week or once a fortnight, providing you choose to give them your undivided attention at the time you say. It validates them and makes them feel important. Do this for each of your children. It boosts their confidence, and the confirmation helps guide their brain to get to grips with the complexities of learning and living.

Best Results Come When You Remember These Points

Always bear in mind the following when you are working with your child or thinking about their needs:

- They are born fully equipped and designed for human development. Growth and learning happen automatically.

- They are naturally intelligent, without any help from anyone.

- They have no idea what this world is like or what their purpose is.

- They are keen to grow and learn. This creates a natural drive to succeed.

- They have no frame of reference for this world.

- Nature's rules work according to growth and development and are full of facts. Your child intuitively understands and trusts these rules.

- The 21st century culture has a set of cultural rules based on profit, gain, and loss and is full of people acting on opinion.

- This means contradiction, and even shock, are inevitable at some point as your child gains in age and experience. You can limit the negative effect of this by educating and building resilience in your child.

- Your child is not meant to change themselves to 'fit in' to the world. But they don't know that. So, they might try to be 'like everyone else'. Remind them often that they were designed to be unique, and the world is like a playground of experiences they choose from to develop themselves and their skills.

- Young children are based in feeling. Their brains do not have the reference or language to understand their experience. This means they *can't* always explain their behaviour and, when you ask 'why?', they will shrug their shoulders and look away (or down, usually).

- They are particularly sensitive to your reactions to them, your tone, authenticity, and language.

- They may not feel confident to ask questions in a world where 'everyone' – including you – appears to be behaving as though 'this is how it's meant to be'.

- Young brains can only process seven words at a time – this means keeping instructions short and clear. (This may explain why things you ask them to do or get, don't get done or got!)

- Neural connections are made in the brain through experiences (looking, hearing, walking, talking, moving, etc.).

- Everything we engage in and do repeatedly develops pathways that the brain will wrap with a protein coating called myelin. This makes the skill automatic.

- Experience is invaluable for learning. This means their brain will create stronger, more resilient, pathways when they are actively doing 'real' things.

- Your child's hearing and vision are crucial to their brain development.

- Good hearing is vital to the process of language development, including phonics. Keep an eye on 'glue ear', colds, catarrh, etc.

- Even a family holiday can compromise learning. If your child flies overseas, their hearing can be adversely affected for up to 3 weeks because of the cabin pressure in the plane.

- If you haven't heard of it, multi-sensory learning – which means using more than one of the senses in an activity – is actively used and promoted for children diagnosed with special needs; however, experience has shown multi-sensory learning is of benefit to all children because it uses more connections for the brain to cement the learning. Making learning practical is the key. For example, don't just look at pictures and talk about an elephant; go and see an elephant when possible. That way, your child's brain gets the sight of it, the smell of it, a good sense of the size of it, and the sound of it. Language opportunities increase with practical learning as well.

- They need your confirmation and feedback, to let them know they're on the right track. Brains process a lot during a day.

- Your feedback helps trigger processes in the brain that secure the pathways being created.

- Your child is fine tuned to what's 'real'. Sarcasm, even 'jokingly used', confuses them and damages their confidence.

- They have no idea what a 'silly question' is...their self-esteem and confidence shrink when they're told they've asked one.

- When your child meets contradiction, it creates pressure from outside. Your child's defence will be to show a change in behaviour. Many parents report seeing this when their child starts school.

- 'Going through the motions' with any work is pointless – a negative attitude, reluctance, tiredness, or not feeling great can all prevent learning.

- Attitude is everything! Let's make them happy, purposeful, and loving learning!

The birth of a baby is the birth of a brain!

The second a child is born, its brain, which has roughly 86 billion neurons, 'hits the ground running', making connections through baby's senses and experience. This is an automatic process.

Every

    single

        sound,

            touch,

                taste,

                    sensation,

                        smell,

                            change of temperature, and

                                movement –

                                    every

                                        single

                                            one –

                                                creates a neural connection.

Newborn brains are busy!

It is tiring. So, they sleep a lot!

All these connections are building a reference bank of experience.

In the first three years, the connections the brain makes have risen to 1,000 trillion.

The important thing to remember here is that the brain has no idea whether the connections it is making are helpful for life or not.

90% of brain development is complete by the age of 5 years

The world presents a feast of experiences, which excites the brain, because it's keen to learn. But without intervention from parents and teachers it cannot make decisions about what it is learning.

Deciding where to start

It helps to find out a little about how your child works when they're learning and what sort of help they need, so here are some activities to help you find out where to start.

Set aside an afternoon to do all of them at once or do them one at a time; it doesn't matter. What matters is that you find the information you need to help your child be the best they can be.

Activities for assessing how your child learns

1. The Timeline – an activity for parents on their own
2. Juggling
3. Memory of random shapes
4. Listening
5. Memory of known shapes
6. Writing
7. Reading – there is more on this in the next book, coming soon!

The activities work best if you give simple instructions, so your child is clear what they need to do, then you watch and listen very carefully.

Let them say or write what they need to say or write, without interrupting, leading, or judging what they say.

Your child is very sensitive, intelligent, and creative. They may also be secretly worried or frightened to say anything because they don't know what will happen if they're honest. You might remember some *confusion* or contradiction from your own childhood.

Real Life Example 3

As a capable 7-year-old, I was sent to a neighbour I didn't know very well to get some sweet peas. She handed me the scissors and waved me towards the end of the garden, telling me to 'help myself'. I didn't know what 'sweet peas' were but felt as though I should...so I guessed and took all her green beans.

Everyone laughed.

It was the first embarrassment I remember in life. It was the first assault on my confidence. None of the adults realised that at the time, so no one explained why they were laughing. These seemingly small but potentially significant incidents can build up over time and cause children to lose confidence and withdraw.

Your child's greatest fear is that you will be disappointed with them, but they haven't got the language skills or the experience to be able to tell you.

Your child needs to feel completely safe when they're being honest. We all know the world is a very contradictory place. Your child sees this too, and it's one of the main reasons they get into difficulty. Remember, there are two sets of rules – one is based in natural growth and the other based in the culture.

What they don't know is that you *do* know the world isn't right, and that you will understand, even if you don't immediately know what to do or say to help.

Avoid assumption or telling them what they know – it may only be what you *think* they know.

> **Real Life Example 4**
> I've met 9-year-old children who lack confidence and struggle to read because they don't know how to break down words, but everyone thinks – and tells them – they're a 'good reader' so they don't say anything.
> Their brain then thinks all 'good readers' struggle to break down words. They think that's what 'good reading' is all about. The best way to fix their confidence is by finding out what the real difficulty is and fixing that.

Let's get real and stop pretending. Children *do* need our help. Now, more than ever.

Even if you feel a little overwhelmed and don't know what to do when you discover what your child needs, we have insights and solutions in this book and online that may help you.

To get you going, here is an activity for parents.

The Timeline

To start us off, we need to look at the timeline of your child's life from birth to now.

It helps to write it down, so you will need a writing utensil.

Only you will see it, unless you want to share it, so, take a break, maybe get a drink, and spend a little time reflecting. A template for this activity follows.

It helps if both parents reflect on the events in your own lives, as well as your child's, since they came into the world.

We do this because life today can be eventful.

Major stress events for you and your family could include:

- The death of someone close
- Separation or divorce
- Moving home
- Emigrating
- Changing jobs
- Stress at work – including bullying
- Money problems
- Chronic illness or injury (or postnatal depression)

Major stress events for your child could include the effect of some of the above in the people around them, but also:

- Separation from a parent or parents – for a period of time or permanent
- Birth of a sibling (how did they react?)
- Starting school
- Learning difficulties
- Learning more than one language
- Changing school
- Friendships
- Bullying
- Death of a pet

Start with the day they were born. Reflect on that event. Here are some questions to help you.

- Were they born on their due date, premature, or late?
- How was everyone affected?
- Was it a normal delivery or caesarean?
- How were they at birth? Were they healthy? Distressed? Did they need any immediate intervention? Remember, children are based in feeling. If their birth was stressful, they will have needed to recover. It is a traumatic event.
- And how were you? Any issues?
- Did they reach all the expected milestones?

Unexpected changes can be forced on families. It isn't right or wrong, it just is! While these events and changes may not appear to directly involve your child, they will be processing the feelings and pressures surrounding them. This can and does impact on their learning and development.

You might be surprised to learn that it takes at least three years for a human being to process a major stress event. For a young child whose brain is developing neural pathways, interruptions and diversions from their natural line of development can arrest the process or disperse it.

After the Coronavirus pandemic, we heard in the UK that very young children returned to school after months-long lockdowns with compromised language skills, as though they have gone backwards. Clearly, the neural pathways that had been developing before the pandemic were not fully formed, had not been 'sealed' in myelin by the brain, so they 'dissolved' and needed to be re-instated. That's okay, as long as we are aware of the process and take this into consideration when planning what the child needs.

By looking at a child's timeline, we can see where any difficulty – if there is difficulty – is likely to have started, and then we can take action to compensate for the change.

By looking at what education expects at the same time, we can see what we might need to do at any given stage to help your child stay bright and developing helpful skills and knowledge for their life.

Now it is time for you to reflect and make a timeline and mark the major events of your child's life on it. You can do that on the template that follows.

Template for Timeline Review

Remember, you do not need to share this with anyone. It is your choice.

Birth to present timeline for   (child's name)

Birth:

Before 1st birthday: Significant events for you and/or your child

   Home:

   Life:

   Health:

Between 1st and 2nd birthday: Significant events for you and/or your child

    Home:

    Life:

    Health:

Between 2nd and 3rd birthday: Significant events for you and/or your child

    Home:

    Life:

    Health:

Between 3rd and 4th birthday: Significant events for you and/or your child

    Home:

    Life:

    Health:

Do this for each year of your child's life.

When you review how life affected your child at any given time, you're in a better position to be able to see the experience and reference their brain will have and what they will have needed to process. This will help you to interpret and understand their current needs and where they might benefit from a little extra help from you.

Whatever is happening to a child 'right now' is where their brain will focus. They will not be able to resume focus on their learning until the brain has processed (settled) the changes that have occurred.

Below are three examples of situations that have affected children's progress and taken the focus off their learning.

Example 1

The concern: At 9 years old, Nathan appeared to be slower than his peers in school. His creative writing, speaking, listening, and comprehension were all affected.

Looking at his timeline, from birth to 5 years Nathan had a Chinese nanny. She spoke to him in Mandarin. At 4 years old he started going to an English nursery. This was when he started to learn English as well and began operating in two languages.

During the first 5 years, our brains create the labyrinth of neural pathways that form the foundation for language. If a child is learning more than one language before this time, it can cause a perceived delay, slowing down their progress in comparison with their peers.

This does not mean that children should only speak one language. What it does mean is that, when the language foundation is being created, the brain needs to be clear which language is the first, dominant, language.

The brain is impartial. It does not know what we want but takes its lead from what we show it in our behaviour.

The key to it all is awareness and knowing how it works, so that you can provide the support your child needs.

The apparent weakness in his English comprehension and achievement in school was nothing to do with Nathan's intelligence. These areas had been affected by the delay in language development caused by switching between languages as the brain was creating those connections. By providing short, intensive 1-2-1 language support for a few months, Nathan's brain was able to fill out the parts of the language he had missed at an early age, and he was soon able to catch up with his peers.

Example 2

The concern: When James was 10 years old, his mum asked for help. His handwriting was of concern – it was illegible – and his poor concentration was stopping him from doing well in school.

We looked at the events that had occurred in James's life. All was fine until James was just over 2 years old. One night, after James had gone to bed, his father left home.

James woke the next day to a major transformation in his world. Mum was naturally in shock and suffering grief; Dad was no longer part of his world.

Experiences like James's are not unique in life today. A young brain takes time to process shock events because it lacks reference. This can occupy the brain and can arrest progress in learning because the brain's focus shifts to what is currently happening. Reconnecting with 'work' must wait. This process takes time.

After explaining how habits develop, James needed a few simple changes he could make, so he could be proud of his handwriting. James was thrilled. His brain re-focused on getting more success in his learning and life and, within six weeks, he was thriving again.

Human beings are natural healers. There is no need to focus on the events themselves, unless more reference is needed or the child is so badly traumatised by an extreme event they need additional therapeutic support. The brain will work it out, but it takes time.

Example 3

The concern: Olga arrived in our Year 5 class part way through the school year. She had arrived in the UK with only her mother. They were refugees. Both had fled a difficult situation and were traumatised. They were without their husband and father.

Olga had joined our school within days of arriving from overseas, and it was thought (correctly) that a routine would help her to settle. She didn't speak a word in school at all for six months.

She was 'adopted' by several of the other children who led her around for the first few weeks and communicated cheerfully through play and a form of sign language. She was monitored carefully by the adults, without intervention.

One day, six months after she arrived, Olga started to speak English – fluently. Her brain had clearly been absorbing the language from the environment, her teachers, and the children in the playground. She was a very bright girl and, despite her previous experiences, was determined to do well in school and quickly caught up.

The only adult intervention in Olga's case was 'care from a distance' – making sure the environment was a safe and supportive one while her brain and systems processed all they needed to process to bring her back to herself and allow her to settle.

How life events can affect children's learning

Traumatic events like this are increasingly common in the culture we've inherited in the 21st century. They have become part of our life experience and impact all of us, including the young.

Children's brains don't know this and can be diverted from their focus on formal learning when such events or experiences happen in their own life. Their brain is trying to deal with the 'new information' for which they may have no reference.

When a child is overwhelmed, just like any of us, it takes time to rebalance and reconnect. As adults, we have learnt more strategies and ways to help ourselves deal with overwhelm and negativity. Your child will not have these references or strategies, nor the communication skills to talk to you at length about it.

Children are born for growth and development. Negativity creates a contradiction.

The added complication is that we live in an 'instant' world, where expectations are high, and we live at a faster pace than is natural to us.

Whatever challenges you and your children have experienced, there is safety and certainty in knowing that, although the world may cause disruption and stress, one thing is never going to change – our core learning and development needs.

Human beings are do-ers!

Children are born looking forward to doing.

Their brain, two thirds 'empty', waits to be educated and, without intervention, will be *automatically* educated by experience, by trial and error, or by luck, which we know can be dangerous in a chaotic world.

Whether or not you and your child have been distracted by events you have experienced, working on these skills will focus your child by prioritising their innate need for growth and personal development and you can use their experiences in the world to help you do that.

Research has shown that to be our most effective as human beings, we need to develop 'executive function' skills. Don't be put off by the name! You have all these skills. Some you will be brilliant at, some maybe not so brilliant, but you will not be a stranger to them.

Here is a list of the Executive Function Skills we all need:

- Self-control
- Focus and attention
- Organisation
- Memory (especially working memory)
- Planning
- Time management
- Critical thinking
- Task initiation
- Perseverance
- Flexibility

We are all born with the potential to develop these skills in time, but they are not specifically taught as part of the curriculum in school, even though they are critical for effective learning and, one way or another, are essential for all we do in life.

Let's see how your child is getting on with some activities that help you discover their specific needs.

JUGGLING!

Can you?

Do you?

Does your child?

You're missing a trick without it!

Assessment Activity 1: Juggling

Reasons to juggle:

- It shows you how well your child can follow instructions – needed for school.
- It improves their hand-eye coordination – needed for handwriting, drawing, and other learning.
- It exercises the part of their brain that does mental maths, too.
- Juggling needs their brain to focus and concentrate – like a lot of what happens at school.
- It's fun. They love it!
- They can get a success at a time in their life when they think there's not much they *can* do.

Rough guide to expectations – children vary. You will need to help them.

- Use a medium to large, light ball to start (like a beach ball).
- From 18 months – teach rolling and pushing a ball.
- 3 years-ish – aim for catching a medium-sized ball with both hands.
- 4/5 years – aim to throw and catch using both hands.

Continue developing the skill:

- Throw into the air and catch using both hands.
- Throw into the air and catch using one hand.
- When they can do this, introduce a second ball.

Instructions need to be simple, and you need to show them. Young brains see a person juggling and think they need to throw both balls at the same time. They need you to show and tell them.

Their brain is busy but loves learning a skill. To be able to juggle, your child's brain must do all these new things:

- Coordinate throwing
- Listen and process information
- Get their posture ready
- Estimate strength of throw needed
- Focus
- Judge distance
- Get hands in position to catch
- Judge speed of ball...and more

There's a lot going on inside their brain so use as few words as possible to avoid overwhelm. Start like this:

- Ask them: Which is your throwing hand? If they're not sure, suggest the hand they use to write and draw.
- Tell them: *Always* use that hand to throw. (Their brain may not know it needs to decide, so help it.)
- Tell and then show: Throw the ball straight up to a bit higher than your head.
- Tell and then show: While the ball is in the air, pass the second ball into your throwing hand.
- Tell and then show: Catch the first ball with your catching hand.
- Tell them: You'll watch while they 'have a go'... no pressure, please.

Don't forget to give feedback. It's essential if you want to get the most from this simple activity.

Their brain is processing a lot of information. It cannot do feedback fast enough yet. They need you to watch and give feedback such as:

- Too high
- Too low
- Too far over
- Too far forward

- Don't throw it backwards
- Perfect! Again. (always build on a success)
- Stand up straight
- Wait until your body is ready (very common need while they learn self-control – another 'executive function')
- YES! (when they get it right – brain needs to know)
- Too strong
- More oomph!
- Not over your head; above your head
- YES, brilliant, well done!

As their brain gets the hang of it, they get excited. All this can happen in just 10 minutes and is so beneficial to your child's overall learning and development.

When to juggle

Here's a little guide to what to say and do to really make the most of this activity.

To fully engage, children's brains need to understand why they are doing something and what you want them to get from it, so their brain focuses on that particular benefit.

Examples follow.

Before school: 'Let's help your brain get ready to focus. Let's have a 2-minute juggle!'

After school: 'Let's get your brain ready for homework with a few juggles!' – one minute (timed) – 'How many can you do without dropping the ball?'

What's important is the burst of fun and the quick win before study.

When their brain gets tired doing a homework assignment: 'Okay – Brain Break! – 20 juggles, off you go.' If they drop the ball, they can start at 1 again until the goal is achieved.

What's important is the brain refresh by breaking the study. This works between homework subjects, to reset the brain.

Quick, purposeful bursts of juggling can be beneficial for your child's learning and sense of fun and achievement.

GAIL HUGMAN

A 3-minute memory challenge!

Inspired by work in 'Improve Your Memory' by Robert Allen

Assessment Activity 2: Random Shapes – A 3-Minute Memory Challenge

You will need:

- A printed copy of the Random Shapes test
- A three-minute timer
- Some blank paper
- Pencil

What to do:

- Give your child a copy of the Random Shapes Test.
- Tell them, 'We are going to see how well your brain remembers things, so that we can find out how to help it get better at it.'
- Do not give any help or tips about *how* to do it. This will give you the opportunity to watch how they approach new and unfamiliar things at school.
- Tell them they have three minutes to look at the shapes and try to remember as much as they can. If they want to, they can copy the shapes or make notes on some paper.
- Ask if they are ready and, when they are, turn on the timer.
- At the end of three minutes, tell them to stop.
- Remove any notes or drawings.
- Ask them to draw what they remember.

Random shapes

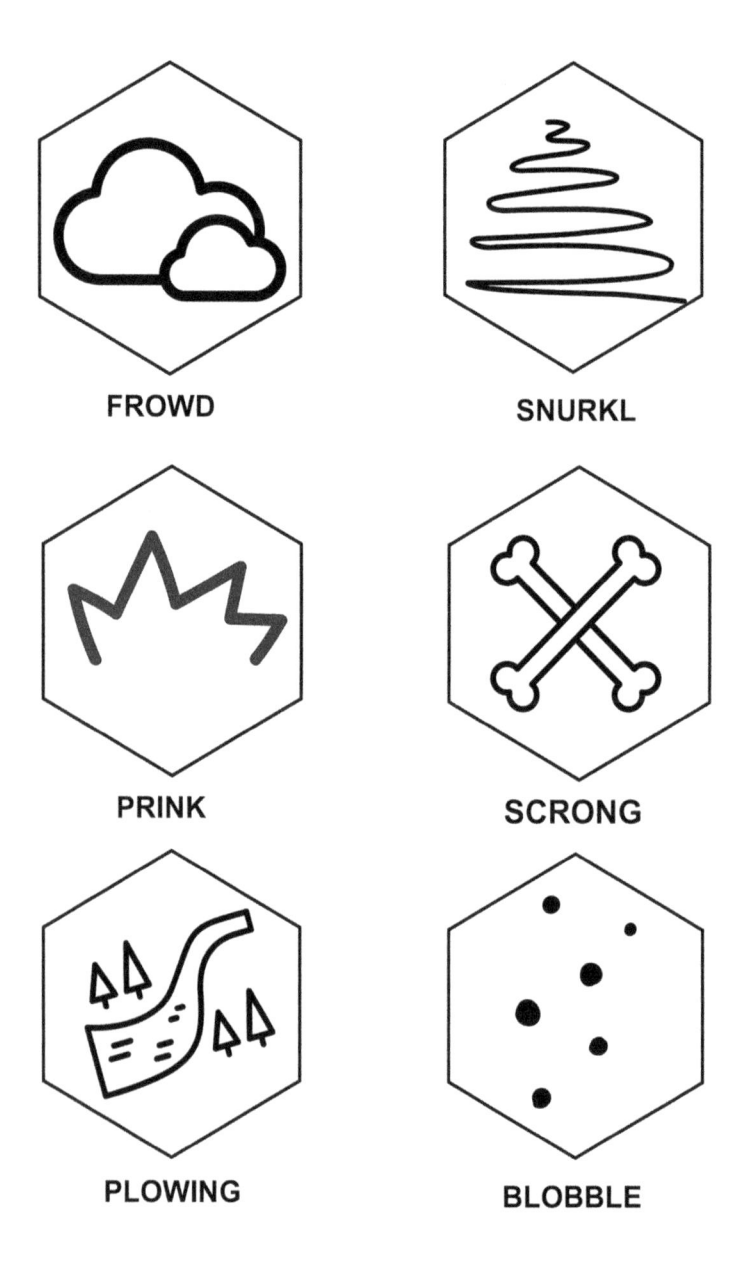

FROWD

SNURKL

PRINK

SCRONG

PLOWING

BLOBBLE

There is no time limit for drawing what they can remember. They will most likely say when they have finished.

When your child tells you they have finished, here are some questions to ask if they haven't remembered some of the items (which is likely):

- How many boxes were there?
- Can you remember any of the words?

You may both be surprised when they tell you there were six boxes, especially if they haven't drawn six boxes.

This helps you point out that their brain knows more than they think.

It's helpful to let them know that if they count the boxes first, then draw six boxes in their notes before putting in the shapes, it will help their brain remember more.

This activity shows you how your child approaches unfamiliar objects and gives you insight into what they need to help them.

The next activity shows you what their brain does when they are asked to remember known items.

Assessment Activity 3: Memory – Known Objects

You will need:

- A printed copy of the Known Objects test
- A one-minute timer
- Some blank paper
- Pencil

What to do:

- Give the Known Objects sheet to your child and tell them (their brain) that you want to see how well their memory works with things they know.
- Ask them to name everything they can see to check they can identify each object.
- Give them the blank paper and pencil.
- Tell them they are going to have one minute to look at all the objects and do whatever they need to do to remember them. Don't make any suggestions at this point if you want to know how well your child remembers things on their own.
- Tell them that at the end of one minute, you will take away the sheet and any notes they have made and will ask them to write or draw what they remember. Let them know you are not going to worry about spelling or handwriting as long as you can understand what

they've written. Younger children (5–7 years) can simply tell you what they remember, and you can write for them.

From this activity you can see how your child approaches work in school.

- Do they look at the whole task first?
- Do they count all the items, so their brain knows what it's aiming for?
- Do they group things together?
- *Could* they group things together?

When you have finished observing what they do, this activity can be used to show them different ways to help their brain organise information for future use.

Gail Hugman

Known objects

Assessment Activity 4: Short-Term Memory – Listening

For this activity, you need approximately 15 minutes uninterrupted time with your child. You can do this exercise with all school-age children from aged 6 years.

- Tell your child, 'Let's see what happens in your brain when you do your best listening. I'm going to read a short story and you need to do your best listening. At the end, I'm going to ask you twelve questions. I can read the story twice if you like, but once I start to ask the questions, you won't be able to hear the story again. Get comfortable. Let me know when you're ready for me to start reading.'

- Read the following story, slowly and clearly. When you have finished reading, ask your child if they'd like to hear it again or if you should ask the questions. (These follow the story.)

Sometimes, children who don't do well with the visual memory exercises will do exceptionally well with the listening exercise. This will let you know that they are more likely to rely on their listening in school. This will also be very useful information for their teacher, who can then ensure that they are focused and listening when their lesson begins.

The story is modelled on one from Robert Allen's book *Improve Your Memory*, a fabulous resource for anyone wanting to delve further into developing their memory.

The story

Roger, Pete, and I always like to plan our trips out together. Planning it makes us feel we've had twice the fun. The baby, Catherine, isn't old enough yet to join us.

We usually go in the car, but it was in the garage, so we decided to go on the bus. We could catch the number 31 there because it ran on Tuesday mornings, and we arranged to meet at the bus stop in time for the 10:20 a.m. into Marbrey bus station.

The plan was to go to the library first, then the bike shop, and finally the bakery. Pete's great-aunt worked in the bakery, so we always hoped for a treat, and some cupcakes to take home for Catherine and her mum, Roberta.

We would wait at the bus station with our bike transfers, cupcakes, and library books for the 3:30 p.m. number 27 home because the 31 didn't run on Tuesday afternoons.

Questions for listening activity

1. How many boys like to go out?
2. Name two of the boys.
3. What is the name of the baby?
4. Why can't they go out in the car?
5. Where were they planning to go?
6. What number bus did they catch to go into Marbrey?
7. When does the number 31 bus run?
8. Where did they get off the bus?
9. Which three places did they plan to visit?
10. Who worked at the bakery?
11. What did they take home for Catherine and her mum?
12. Why didn't they go home on the 31 bus?

This listening exercise gives you the opportunity to observe what happens when your child does their 'best' listening.

- Did they fidget or were they focused?
- How long were they focused?
- Were they easily distracted or quickly bored?
- Could they recall the answers to the questions?

By looking at how your child behaves when they are on their own with you in this activity you will gain some insight into how they are likely to behave in their class when their teacher is speaking to all the children. It provides the opportunity for you to give your child tips for improving their success at school.

Identifying your child's core needs by interpreting their behaviour

Another useful way to approach your child's development needs is by looking at their behaviour.

If your primary+ aged child shows any of these behaviours…

- Starts work, gets sidetracked and gives up
- Forgets homework or books
- Has tantrums
- Gets stuck when shown a new approach to maths
- Their desk, room, or bag is messy
- Watches what other children are doing before they start work
- Reacts badly to change – especially unexpected (impromptu) change

- Practises avoidance
- Forgets instructions
- Has difficulty getting started on a project
- Calls out in class
- Runs out of time in exams
- Finds maths word problems 'hard'
- Doesn't know what to write

...you are looking at weakness in the core learning skills or attitude.

Parents and teachers rely on these skills developing as children mature; however, the evidence suggests that in the present culture, making your child aware of these skills engages them in their own development, which means they can:

- Appreciate they don't have to wait to 'grow up' before they can do anything – this nourishes their core sense of purpose, which pleases them and their brain.
- Understand what they are meant to be growing in themselves.
- Realise that they need to be involved in developing these skills – it is part of 'their job' (they love that, too!).
- Be held accountable for their behaviour, which means more self-control, more praise, and more confirmation, which everyone appreciates.

The parent role is ideal for giving definition and examples: set realistic targets, monitor, and give feedback.

The feedback you give to your child's brain when you see what they do is crucial. Your child (and their brain) is encouraged when they know they are creating the correct neural pathways. Your congratulation is confirmation that helps to trigger the brain's myelin process, which wraps the pathway and makes the behaviour automatic.

Although it may not happen every time they're learning a new skill, you can know this process has occurred when your child tells you, 'I've got it now!' or you see the realisation and delight on their face when the penny drops, and they radiate confidence.

Feedback is:

A facial expression

A look

A hug

A pat on the back

A smile

Something you say.

A young brain can process seven words at a time – keep feedback short.

This book focuses on how to teach your child the first six of these skills, which develop in the primary years.

- Self-control – includes listening and self-discipline
- Attention – includes focus and concentration
- Working Memory
- Organisation
- Time Management
- Planning

The additional four skills develop independence from puberty, when significant developmental changes occur. Parents and teachers will encourage these when children are younger, but from puberty, children will begin to internalise and initiate them further, to increase independence.

- Task initiation
- Flexibility
- Meta cognition (reflection, evaluation, planning, monitoring)
- Perseverance

Your child needs to know that the primary years are when important skills grow and develop. They need to be taught that a skill is something we *do*, which means we can get better at it with practise. This is important if we know that we're going to need that skill to be the best we can be.

One way to start the discussion is to tell your child that they are in training to be an adult. Part of their job as a child is to learn skills so that they can be independent and do things for themselves. Give them a copy of the following chart.

Scores for Skills

Skill	Score now	Score in 3 months
Self-control		
Attention		
Working Memory		
Organisation		
Time Management		
Planning		

Use the chart to talk a little bit about each skill and define it. Give examples of where we need to use each skill. Give examples to your child of where they particularly need to use the skills. Remember that it may be the first time ever that your child has heard of them, and new information can be tiring.

For children from 7 years on, ask them to give themselves a mark out of 10 for how strong they think they are in each skill. Tell them you will also have a copy and will put a mark out of 10 to show how you see them.

If your child thinks they are 10 out of 10 excellent at self-control, but they don't listen to you when you take them out on trips, or their school report asks them not to call out in class, your mark may be 6 out of 10 – this will give you the basis for a chat about how they can improve it further.

The feedback you give must be impartial and constructive. You need to be able to give them evidence of the behaviour they are aiming to control.

Spend the next week (or two) focused on that one thing. Encourage. Give feedback. Create opportunities for them to practise.

Tell them you're going to help them with some practical activities and, at the end of a week or two, or a month (you choose together), you will review their progress and choose a different skill to work on.

Here are some definitions and activities for your child's brain – you may have better ones from your own experience. Feel free to use those.

Self-Control
Sample introductory talk to have with your child

When we're born, we don't know anything about the world. We have feelings so we can start to learn. We use our feelings to tell us about whether things are good or not. Feelings help us all our lives, but we need to understand what they're telling us.

To start with, we just react to every feeling. But when our brains have more information, we can learn to interpret feelings and make decisions about our reactions.

This means you don't have to react to everything inside you or outside you.

Some children call out in class because they don't have very good self-control. Having self-control is a sign of maturity, but you will see even some adults struggle with self-control sometimes.

What your child needs to know

Self-control is when you take charge inside yourself and, instead of reacting to what you feel, you decide what you want your response to be. Humans are the only creatures that can do this.

You might need to explain this several times, to help your child's brain make the neural connections using its own experience and references, rather than yours.

To help your child make the connections, ask them what they think about behaviour they see when people use self-control and when they don't. Talk about events in their lives to start with – their friends and school:

- What is it like when children call out in class?
- How does your teacher react?
- How does it affect you?
- What do you think when people 'take over' in the playground?

Use examples you know your child has witnessed.

Fun activities to help teach your child self-control

Remember to tell your child that the activity will help them to show their brain that they want to practise being in charge and taking control. By telling them this you get the full benefit of the games.

Every time you use one of these activities, remember to tell your child what they are focusing on. By doing this, their brain knows to 'run' and strengthen that neural path.

Children will love doing these anyway, but if you don't tell them what they are trying to achieve, you won't necessarily get the learning you hope.

Activity 1: Grandmother's footsteps

One person is grandma, and they stand facing away from everyone at the end of the garden or room.

Everyone else lines up at the other end of the garden or room and tries to sneak up on grandma without being seen or heard.

Every now and then, grandma turns around to try to catch someone moving.

The winner is the person who can tap grandma's shoulder before she spots them!

The winner becomes grandma for the next game.

Activity 2: The Voice Game

Shout as loud as you can for one minute, then be silent for one minute! (Children love this – adults, not so much!) Be accurate with the timer; brains get a sense of time from this.

Activity 3: 10 Steps and Change

Decide on a destination. It could be the end of the road where you live, a route in the local park, or the route to school. Tell your child they are going to run 10 steps, then walk 10 steps, then run 10 again and walk 10 steps until they reach the destination. They're doing this to teach their brain to stop when they decide.

Activity 4: Brain Challenge

Explain to your child that you are going to ask them twenty questions, but the answers YES and NO are banned.

They are going to teach their brain to slow down and think of an alternative answer.

Give them an example such as: Are you a boy? Instead of 'yes' or 'no', tell them this could be answered as, 'I am a boy' or 'I am not a boy'. Make sure they understand what is going to happen. Ask twenty questions where the answer mustn't be YES or NO.

Example questions:

- Are you a boy?
- Are you a girl?
- Do you live in this house?
- Am I your mum/dad?
- Did you have breakfast today?
- Is the wall painted blue?
- Can you see out of the window?
- Do you go to school?
- Is this your home?

Special mention in self-control: LISTENING

Listening isn't listed specifically as one of the executive function skills, but as it is so important, we are including it in this section on self-control. Good listening skills are fundamental to brain development and learning.

Like focus and concentration, listening is a skill that children cannot 'see', so their brain can only copy the behaviour, not the skill itself.

If children cannot see the skill, we need to help them experience and understand it by teaching it to them explicitly. This means explaining what happens inside your brain when you are doing it (it's not so hard when you get the hang of it).

If your child's school report suggests they improve their listening, talk to them about what they think listening is:

- How is listening different from hearing?
- What do they need to think about and tell their brain to improve their listening in school?
- What do they need to think about and tell their brain to improve their listening at home?

There is more guidance on listening in my previous book *100 Things to Learn before You're 10*.

Here are some questions for you to reflect on if you think your child needs to improve their listening skills.

- Did I get their attention first? (by name, by touch, by being in the same room)
- Have I interrupted a process? (they were concentrating on something else; they were in a conversation)
- Can they hear me? (over headphones, TV, traffic, or ear problems)
- Did I barge into their thoughts? (by shouting from another room)
- Did I stop them and make eye contact first?
- Have I ever explained the difference between hearing and listening?
- Am I speaking too quickly? (very common)

- Am I saying too much? Too many words? (this is a huge problem for many parent/child relationships)
- Am I speaking clearly? (not eating at the same time)
- Have they got time to think about what I have said and to respond?
- Do I frequently make idle threats? (if you say it, do it or they switch off)
- Do I repeat myself over and over again? (say it, mean it, do it!)
- Have I taught them good listening skills?
- Are they sleeping well?
- Does what I'm saying match my body language and what they are feeling from me? (words do not mask what is really going on in us)
- Am I listening?
- Am I being impatient? (causing anxiety in their brain)
- Am I pausing to allow their brain thinking and response time?

We learn

55% of a message's meaning

from the facial expression

38% from how the message is

said

and just

7% from the actual words

spoken!

Benefits of having self-control (to talk to your child about)

- Children with self-control are more popular because people feel safe around them.
- Children with self-control are showing maturity and this impresses people.

Consequences of not controlling your self

- Children who don't have self-control are often the ones who get into trouble more.
- Children who don't have self-control make people around them more uncomfortable because no one knows what they're going to do next.

How to show self-control at school

- One of the best ways to show self-control at school is by listening when your teacher is talking to everyone.
- Avoid talking to your friends when your teacher is talking (even if your friends speak to you, ask them to wait until break).
- If plans change, don't sulk!
- Avoid arguing with your teacher. If they have made

a mistake about you or your work, or you feel something is unfair, you can speak to them or, if you feel too uncomfortable to do that, it's something a parent can help with so talk to them.

How to practise self-control at home

Choose one thing at a time to focus on. Remember, you need to help their brain make the neural connections that will develop into habits.

- Perhaps you would like your child to be a better listener? Point this out to them and focus on it for a month.
- Tell them when they need to be a better listener. Bedtime? Morning? Homework time? Choose only one to work on.
- Tell them how you will know they have improved. Will they look at you? Stop what they're doing? Answer you?
- Perhaps you would like to see your child react to disappointment better? Point this out and talk about ways they could react to change instead.

Whatever you choose to focus on, your feedback is crucial.

You know your child's habitual reactions, so don't be surprised to see habits appear. But if they lapse, remind them that they said they wanted to focus on self-control, and this is old behaviour that doesn't fit any more.

Each 'success' needs to be confirmed with a 'well done, I noticed you took more self-control there. How do you feel about it? Are you pleased with yourself?'

By taking an active interest in every attempt to take control you will see changes happen more quickly than without your feedback. We all like to be praised when we try.

Real Life Example 5

The parents were worried. Their 8-year-old daughter, Molly, would not dress herself in the morning. Her younger siblings needed their working mother's help to get ready, but she would wait until Mum dressed her and refused to help herself. Tantrums about it were frequent. The situation was frustrating.

With two other younger children, Mum and Dad obviously wanted Molly to be more independent and dress herself in the morning, but she resisted every strategy they had tried.

We spoke to Molly about training to be an adult and the self-control she needed to be growing in herself. We explained that she seemed to be having difficulty getting dressed by herself and asked what was stopping her.

> Molly tearfully explained that her mum gave her a cuddle every time she dressed her. She thought that if Mum stopped dressing her, cuddles would stop.
>
> We told her that she would get even bigger cuddles if she dressed herself because Mum would be so pleased to see her taking control. Molly became more independent with greater self-control overnight.

Boost the power of any activity by telling your child what they are learning from it, so their brain knows what neural pathways it is making.

Focus and Attention

Sample introductory talk to have with your child

The world is colourful, interesting, busy, and noisy. There's a lot of interruption and distraction for your brain. This means you need to be able to take charge in yourself and not let your brain be distracted by what's happening around you, or other people's behaviour, when you have important things to do for yourself and your own life.

Brains work best in quieter spaces when there isn't too much to distract them. You can help your brain do a better job for you when you know this.

What your child needs to know

- When we focus, we use all our energy to look at or think about one thing. We don't think about anything else when we are concentrating. (It is best to give this definition when your child is fully concentrating so that their brain can marry the knowledge with the feeling of concentration.)

- This experience is a crucial part of the process for understanding.

Real Life Example 6

I met David when he was 11 years old. He didn't concentrate well at school and was not doing well in his studies.

Around the edge of the grass in his garden there was a narrow rim of decorative bricks, separating the grass from the path. I asked David if he could walk on this around the edge of the grass. He thought this was funny and found it tricky to keep his balance on the narrow path at first. He was encouraged to persevere and gradually mastered the balancing and slow steps needed to follow it.

While he was completely focused on this, he (his brain) was told that what he was 'now feeling' we call concentration.

David did this activity every day for a week. He was encouraged to say quietly in his head, 'I am walking the path of focus and concentration' as he did it.

He became very good at this activity and then transferred it to walking up the driveway of his school, telling himself quietly that he was 'walking the path to focus and concentration'. David's focus in the classroom improved. He was able to achieve more and was much happier with himself (as were all the adults involved!).

Fun activities to help you teach your child to recognise when they are concentrating

Choose one of the activities below for helping your child with concentration and, when you see your child is fully focused, you can tell them – and therefore their brain – that 'what you are now doing is using all your energy to focus on one thing. We call this concentration.'

Activity 1: The Balance Skill

Ask the child to balance a book on their head and keep it there for at least one minute. Make sure to use a timer. While they are doing this, give them a commentary to advise them to slow down or wait or make some adjustment to keep the balance, and it will help their brain master the skill.

Activity 2: The Water Challenge

Fill a glass to the top with water and ask the child to walk the length of the hallway and back again without spilling a drop.

If you have practised other exercises first, you can start to encourage your child to run their own commentary in their head. 'Tell your brain to help you keep control, so you don't spill any water.' Talk to them about how they managed to stay calm enough inside to achieve the goal.

Activity 3: Advanced Water Challenge

Ask the child to fill up an ice cube tray with water and carry it to the freezer without spilling any water.

Benefits of teaching your brain to concentrate (to talk to your child about)

- You find it easier to understand what you need to do at school.
- Your brain has the chance to make connections from learning.
- Your teachers will notice that you are trying hard, which attracts positive energy to you.
- Tests and exams are easier to do because you know your brain has the information that you've been taught.
- This makes you more confident.
- You feel more mature, and self-respect grows.

Consequences of weak concentration

- If you don't focus on what is being taught to you, your brain can't fully make the connections you need.
- This makes it stressful when you start to do tests and exams.
- Your teacher will not be able to do their job of teaching so easily because they will need to keep reminding you.

How to show concentration at school

- Teachers work hard to give you information and activities to help you understand the world and how things work. You need to listen when your teacher is talking to you.
- You need to concentrate on your work so that your brain has a chance to learn it.
- Save talking to your friends until break time – tell them you are concentrating!

How to practise concentration at home

- No one expects you to concentrate all day.
- When we concentrate, we use a lot of energy and it can be tiring, so we usually concentrate for small amounts of time, but often, during the day.
- At home, you need to concentrate to do your homework or instrument practise, so we need to make a space and time for you to do that.
- Let your child choose one thing to work on where they will make every effort to improve their concentration.

Remember to give feedback to help them recognise when they are getting it right.

Time Management
Sample introductory talk to have with your child

Time is manmade. None of us are born knowing how to tell the time, which means you need to learn about time and how to tell it because of the culture we live in.

There are twenty-four hours in a day.

Do you know when the day starts? (You, the parent, need to check this!)

Everyone has twenty-four hours in their day! People who do well have twenty-four hours in their day. People who don't do well also have twenty-four hours in their day. How we use our time can make the difference.

What your child needs to know

Time management is about taking charge of what you must do and how long you have to do it.

Fun activities to help you teach and practise time management at home

To get better at time management, your child needs to know their limitations and what they are capable of. The following activities help their brain to learn this.

Before doing any of these activities, remember to tell your child the reason they are doing it. Example: 'We're going to teach your brain what you're able to do in one minute, so that you can work out how long things take for you to do.'

Activity: One-minute exercises

- How many times do you think you can write your name neatly in one minute? Estimate, then do it. (Many children overestimate when they start.)
- How many hops can you do in one minute? Estimate, then do it. (Remind their brain of the reason before you do this.)
- The card game Blink is excellent for speeding up thinking skills because, in their wish to win the game, the children push themselves to process information more quickly. Let them know that their brain will learn how to speed up and be better at doing mental maths by playing Blink.
- Dobble or Spot It! are similar games if you cannot find Blink.
- I also recommend getting the game Hue Knew to play if it is still available.
- Any games which require mental manipulation and sorting of information will help to speed up processing.

Benefits of good time management to share with your child

- When you are good at managing time, you get your work done on time.
- Nobody has to keep reminding you to do things because you remember to do them yourself (so teachers and parents are happier!).
- You have more time to spend on the things you like to do.
- You show you are being more responsible for yourself, which attracts respect.
- You can be proud of your achievements because you know you have taken charge of your time and used it well.
- You will find it easier to plan when you know how to manage time.

Consequences of weak time management

- You're always getting told off for wasting time.
- You get into trouble for keeping people waiting.
- You don't get work finished and must do it when everyone else is enjoying themselves.
- You seem immature and as though you can't be given responsibility.

- You can finish up feeling grumpy and unhappy with yourself, which isn't fun for anyone!

How to show time management at school

- Being on time is a good quality to have that will be helpful in life.
- When you get your work done on time and in class, your teacher can help you if you get stuck.
- Teachers have a lot of work to get through and they appreciate it when you are respectful and do your best not to waste time.
- You make it easier for teachers to write positive comments on your report.

How to practise time management at home

You will know the areas where your child needs to manage time better. Focus on only one area to improve at a time.

- Perhaps they could get themselves dressed more quickly in the morning?
- Perhaps they could manage homework time more efficiently?
- Maybe you'd like them to come for their dinner more promptly?

Whatever you choose, it is best to take the time to have a chat with your child about the benefits and consequences of the current situation. Encourage them to choose a weak area to work on. They need to know how their behaviour affects them personally, and how it affects others around them. Focus on the chosen area for at least a week.

Parents need to watch out for progress – if your child is aiming to dress themselves more quickly, giving a gentle reminder as they go to bed will help the brain wake up with that focus.

Giving regular feedback when your child makes even a tiny bit of progress gives their brain the message that they are on the right track. They like that.

Always make sure your child's brain knows why they are doing any activity and what skill they will be getting better at.

Planning

Sample introductory talk to have with your child

We live in a world where it's easy to become overwhelmed because there is so much going on and our brain doesn't know what we want.

Our brain doesn't know anything about the world when we're born. We need to teach it so that it can help us. Our brain doesn't know what's good for us and what isn't, which is why parents and teachers are very important at the beginning.

The adults do most of the planning for us. They tell us when we have to get up, eat, go to school, go to clubs, and do our homework. They do this to help us until we learn to plan for ourselves.

To be good at planning, you need to know what you have to do, as well as what you want to do, and how much time you've got to get everything done.

Fun activities to help you teach and practise planning

To start with, we need to teach your brain what different amounts of time feel like. I recommend using sand timers for this because brains like to see the sand running through, but if you haven't got a sand timer, use any timer that can measure a minute.

- Stand or sit still and watch a one-minute timer run through one minute. This lets your brain know what a minute feels like and is important for when you are working out how long things will take you. You can do this more than once.

    While you are watching the timer run through one minute, estimate how many times you could write your name before the timer ends!

- Now using paper and pencil, set the timer again and write your name (neatly!) as many times as you can to see whether your brain was right. It might have over-estimated or underestimated. It doesn't matter. There is no right answer! What you and your brain need to know is how much you can do in different amounts of time.

- If you set the timer for two minutes, would you double the number of times you can write your name? You can try this too, to find out!

- Set a timer and read for five minutes in your head. Notice how many pages you read. Now read aloud for five minutes to an adult. Did you read more in your head or out loud? This is important information for your brain to know for when you do schoolwork.

- Make a list of all the things you need to do before school. Time yourself getting dressed, packing your bag, eating breakfast, and so on. Doing this helps your brain know exactly how long you need and can help you speed up if you're running out of time.

Benefits of good planning

- You don't get stressed about work because you know when it will get done.
- You always have what you need to do your work, and you feel better prepared. This makes you more confident.
- Teachers know that you're reliable with work.
- You have time for the fun things too!

Consequences of not planning

- You get stressed because you run out of time or forget to do things that you were supposed to do.
- Life feels out of control sometimes and can make you anxious.
- You get into trouble for not doing things you were meant to do.

- You sometimes miss out because you have to catch up.

How to practice good planning at home

- You can plan homework.
- You can plan to help your mum.
- You can plan to help your dad.
- You can plan to help your brother/sister.
- You can plan to tidy your room (then your mum won't have to tell you!).
- Remember your parents know the family 'master plan' – trips to see aunty or grandad, or trips to the zoo – so always check your plans with them to make sure there isn't something you don't know about happening.
- Remember to plan play time and rest times, too.

How to practice good planning at school

- Your work area has everything you need before you start.
- Your work is finished and handed in on time.
- You're always on time for lessons.

Games that can help develop strategic (planning) thinking

Let your brain know that strategic planning is the focus while you play!

- Chess – when you talk about the rules in chess, point out the part of the thinking that is strategic – that means the brain needs to work out the best positions to play, to help you win.
- Monopoly – this is another great game for teaching strategic thinking. Start simple: explain how buying groups of properties gives you the advantage.
- Nubble – this is a board game that is excellent for strategic thinking, practising mental maths, and planning. Recommended for children 7+ years.

Organisation

Sample introductory talk to have with your child

Everything we see, hear, touch, smell, and taste must be processed by our brain. If it is all in a muddle, it makes our brain's job harder – it uses more energy and can make us tired. This can be stressful for us and make us late for things as it tries to make sense of things.

Being organised helps our brain to work efficiently and we feel better. Being organised also helps our brain know how we like information stored and it will be easier to revise for exams.

Imagine if I empty everything out of the cupboards in the kitchen and put it all in a big heap on the worktop! No one would be able to find what they were looking for and it would be very stressful. We organise things to make it easy for our brain to help us and to save time when we are doing things.

Fun activities to help you boost your child's organisation skills

Exercise 1: Sorting

- Get together a collection of shapes. It could be buttons, different shapes, sizes, and colours; or it could be something from their toys – building blocks or Lego pieces.
- Put the shapes into a pile on the table and ask your child to sort them. If they ask how, just repeat the instruction to 'sort them'. Don't give any other help, unless they need reassurance that there is no right or wrong answer.
- Give them as much time as they need to sort them.
- There should be no pressure on them to do this.

This will show you how they react when they have to use their own initiative.

- When they have finished sorting, ask them what criteria they used ('What made you put them into those groups?').
- When they have done this, ask them if there is another way they could sort them.
- Again, give as much time as needed for them to do this without pressure. When they have finished sorting, ask what criteria they used.

Depending on the amount of time you've got for this – we recommend up to half an hour to give your child's brain time to process all the information and sort – you can repeat the exercise until your child tells you they can't think of any other way to sort them. There might be as many as six or seven ways – by colour, by shape, by number of sides, by thickness, and so on.

There are several big lessons in this that you could teach your child, such as:

- Your brain now knows that things can be organised in different ways.
- You now have experience of organising something by yourself.

- You are just as capable as anyone else at organising things.
- We organise things to help us to remember where they are.

Ask your child:

- What was your favourite way of sorting the shapes?
- Was it the first way you thought of, or did you find it after a few tries?

Exercise 2: Organisation

- Take some time to explain how some of the household things are organised, such as the kitchen.
- Explain why things are where they are. Who decided this?
- Ask if they can think of a better way to organise it – they might surprise you!

Exercise 3: Colouring

- Use the page provided below and four crayons of different colours.
- The only instruction is to colour these shapes using only the colours provided and make each shape different.
- Watch to see how systematic your child is.

When they have completed the task, talk about what you observed that was good (if they *were* being systematic) and what you observed that could be improved (maybe they could get just the right number of crayons ready?).

Ask your child what the experience was like for them and whether they would approach it differently if they had to do it again.

- Could they organise the crayons differently to make it easier to remember which one to use next?
- Did they randomly toss the colours aside or were they methodical?

Ask what they learnt from the experience. This helps the brain to consolidate the learning.

Organisation 3

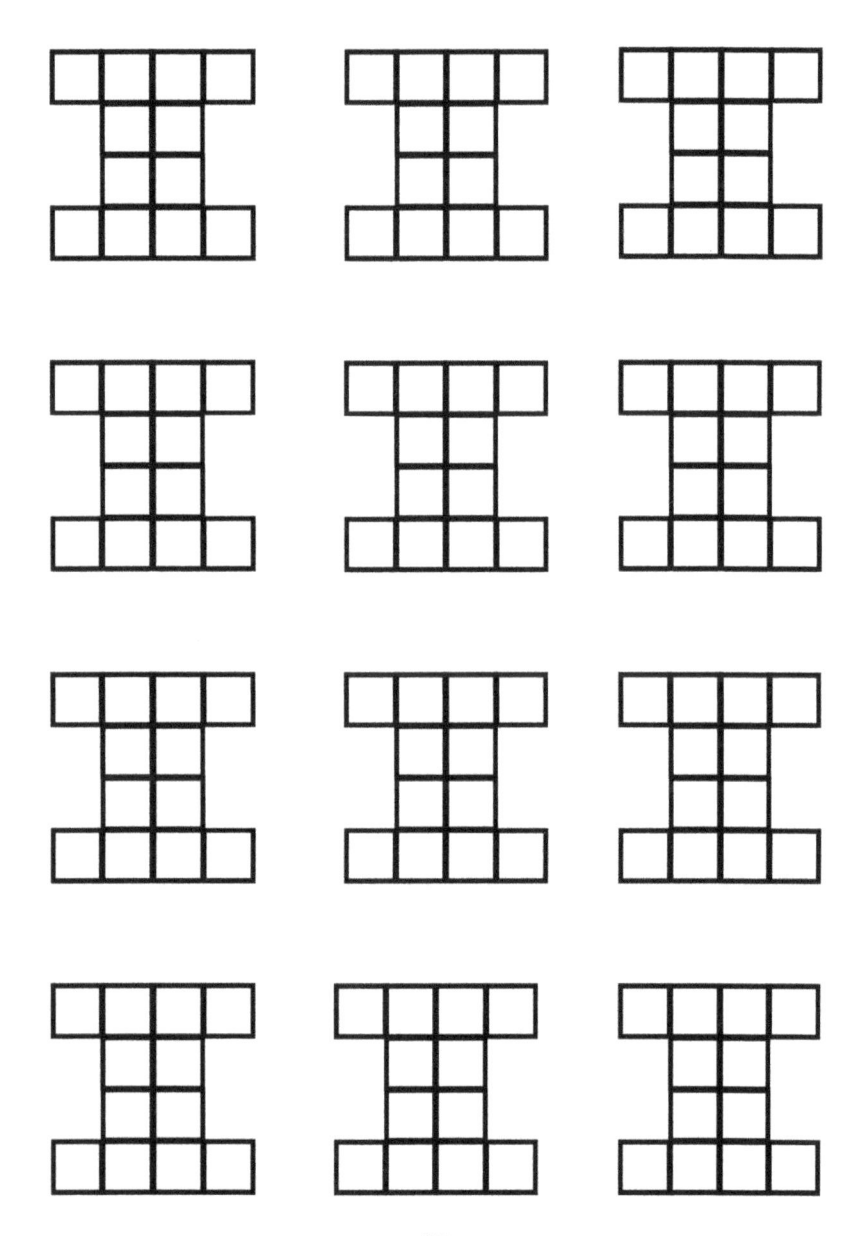

Working Memory

These exercises are great to use with any school-age child up to 12 years old, including neurodiverse children. They are simple, fun, and require few resources. The most important thing is to remember to tell them you are exercising their brain and giving reference to it.

Working memory is like having a Post-It Note in your brain. It is short-term memory, which means your brain isn't meant to hold onto it for very long. For example, it means being able to follow several instructions and work things out while remembering what you're trying to achieve. It is needed for problem solving, and organising what we need to keep in long-term memory.

Working memory is not the same as remembering things from your last holiday, which is usually stored in long-term memory.

You know how frustrating it can be…it's always most obvious when you're in a hurry and you tell your child to 'go upstairs, wash your hands, and bring your jumper down'. And…

Your child has gone upstairs, washed their hands (possibly), then forgotten the other bits, got distracted, and you find them playing with Lego blocks ten minutes later.

Children who regularly forget their bag, their reading book, or their homework are also prime candidates for working memory help.

So, how to start.

Activity 1: Brain Train – Memory

Let your child know what you're about to show them. 'We're going to help your brain improve your working memory.'

Children love fascinating facts because their brain is in reference-building mode. Tell them that you've heard young brains can only remember seven things at a time and suggest you test this out!

- Use a group of small objects. I use small toy animals.
- Show your child the first animal and ask them what they're looking at, e.g., a lion.
- Tell them to keep saying it quietly in their head while you show them the second animal, e.g., a bear.
- The child now has been keeping (lion) in their head and answers 'lion, bear'.
- When you have shown them the second animal, ask them to keep saying the animals they have seen in their head while you show them a third animal, e.g., a giraffe.

- The child now has (lion, bear) in their head, and answers 'lion, bear, giraffe'.
- Keep adding and repeating the full list until you reach seven animals.
- By telling your child to repeat the full list aloud each time, you will be helping to teach their brain to hold on to information by repetition.
- Ask them if they think they can do more…they often want to carry on. According to what they say, keep going until they stop. Children love to push through and try to 'beat' seven. In reality, they can sometimes remember up to 14 animals.
- Vary this activity, using different items.

Activity 2: Brain Train – Pictures for Memory

I use Brainbox memory cards for this activity. You need a simple picture for your child to look at for one minute. You could also use the pictures from a simple colouring book. The subject of the picture isn't important. It can be animals, plants, characters, countries, etc. The important thing is that it is simple and clear.

Tell your child you're going to do a memory activity to teach their brain what to do when their teacher shows them something. This activity will help them learn to focus and recall important information when it's needed.

Tell them that they will have 10 seconds to look at the picture before you ask them 6 pre-prepared questions about it. The Brainbox cards have questions on the back; otherwise, prepare simple questions such as:

- What colour is...?
- How many...?
- Is there a....?
- What is in the background...?

The questions need to focus on small details as well.

Repeat that they have 10 seconds to look at the picture as you give it to them. Use a small timer if you have one – brains often like to see the sand running through.

After 10 seconds, take the card back and ask the questions. Do not correct your child if they get it wrong; move on to the next question. They may get all answers correct; they may not. But in any event, explain that you are going to show them a way to help their brain focus and remember.

Give them another card or image and tell them this time to describe out loud what they are looking at and to make sure their brain is listening at the same time. After they have finished, take the image away and ask the questions.

When they have finished, ask them if they found it easier this time. If they say they did, ask them what they think make the difference; this helps consolidate the information in their brain.

Remind them that when their teacher shows them something at school, they need to tell their brain what they are looking at, so their brain can help them to remember it.

Activity 3: The Shop Game

Tell your child you're going to help their brain learn to keep things they want to remember by playing the Shop Game.

The first person starts by saying, 'I went to the shop, and I bought apples.' The next person must repeat what was said and add an item, so they would say, 'I went to the shop, and I bought apples and bread.'

The next person (or first person again), repeats what has been said and adds another item. Continue until someone forgets what has been bought.

How many items were remembered? Whatever it is, the target is to remember more next time.

Activity 4: Alphabetical Shop Game

A more advanced version of Activity 3 can need items bought to be in alphabetical order! Apples, bread, carrots, dog food, eggs, fish, granola, hairspray, icing, juice, kale...

Neurodiverse children benefit from these exercises and may need additional support with physical links and reminders, such as Post-It Notes in their pencil case or a sticking plaster on the back of their hand to remind them of things they need to do (such as bring homework home.)

If you don't tell your child what they're learning, their brain won't necessarily know what to focus on. It is in reference-building mode.

'Oh! *Now* I get it!'

Everything a human being does – everything – influences their brain.

Not all of it will 'stick'. Everything we engage in and do repeatedly develops pathways that the brain will wrap with a coating called myelin. This makes the skills automatic.

When your child understands that school will teach them about what was here before they arrived, and that they need to use what school gives them to develop themselves, their knowledge, skills, and attitude become positive towards it.

When they know that 'doing maths' is helping to teach their brain to think in different ways – to sort, sometimes to be systematic, and sometimes to reason – and when they learn that persevering with good handwriting is developing their self-control, they more readily engage in the process.

When they can choose, with your help, to develop their creativity this week using their spellings, and perhaps use their spellings next week to develop their memory skills, learning is no longer being done to them.

When they come home and tell you, 'I did it! I focused for the whole of the first lesson and my teacher gave me a star!' and you applaud them for it, the brain takes that as the trigger to produce myelin for that neural pathway and learning becomes an exciting activity, and one you both can use to build on and set a target for the next day.

Your child is yearning for development. They want to get it right! When their behaviour is challenging, rather than trying to take control, give feedback. Ask them if what they're now doing is what they want their brain to keep. They will usually stop, think, and 'autocorrect'.

Instead of scolding your child for delaying homework, you begin to ask, 'What's happening with your self-control?' When they are procrastinating about tidying their things away, remind them that they need to develop their organisation skills.

Tell them if they're being annoying – they might not realise – and ask them if that is what they wanted to be. Remind them that they are in control of it.

Tell your child how things work – especially the things they cannot see, like the skills and processes described in this book. They really do need to know before they mature because making changes is SO much easier as a child.

It is interesting to note that myelin is the substance that breaks down when a person has dementia. The stronger the connections we make, especially during our growth phase as children, the better protected our brains will be in later life. This has been scientifically proven.

> **Real Life Example 7**
>
> A mum once asked how to stop her children 'wrecking' the lounge, which she considered to be her special place. They had a playroom, but they preferred to be in the lounge. It seems she hadn't told them that it mattered to her. When she explained to them that it was special and asked them to help her keep it special, they were more than happy to help – and to play in the playroom!

And finally...a reminder

The one question to bear in mind, whatever your child is doing or learning, is: What is my child *actually* learning from this?

Not what you *think* they're learning. Not what you *hope* they're learning. But what neural pathways are *being* created by their behaviour or work?

Asking this one question will help you to see what will help them in life, and what feedback you need to give to guide them to success.

Just one more thing...

They will need to develop all the skills mentioned before they can successfully develop the final four skills, which are:

- Critical thinking – being able to reflect on and evaluate work, make decisions, and problem solve

- Task initiation – understanding what work needs to be done and organising yourself to do it efficiently

- Perseverance – being able to overcome challenges that may get in the way of achieving a goal

- Flexibility – being able to quickly change thinking from one topic to another

While we can encourage primary-aged children to start to develop these additional skills by the way we give feedback to them, in general, their brains don't have enough reference or experience, and are not mature enough in their processing of information to recognise when they might need them to be applied.

That said, critical thinking can be encouraged through weekly or even monthly 'planned conversations' about how they're getting on, and what they've found interesting or difficult recently.

When you talk about their work, or critique a piece of writing, ask them what they were hoping to achieve and whether they had any difficulty, and how they solved or overcame it. Do they feel they have achieved what they had hoped?

You can also start to encourage them to have a view about things in the news (children's newspapers and magazines can help these days), or where you all go on holiday, or what colour to paint the lounge.

Let them know that their brain needs to learn to evaluate and reflect and that we call this 'critical thinking' while you are talking to them. Critical thinking is a skill that will be tested many times in their life.

Start to talk about taking responsibility for the quality of their own work and behaviour. This is especially important towards the end of primary school.

When they start secondary school, many children face difficulties because their organisation, planning, and study skills are not developed enough. Secondary school, where they move from class to class and a variety of teachers, is so different from primary school that they can be quickly overwhelmed.

Flexibility and perseverance develop when we really want to achieve something. We apply these by knowing what 'the bigger picture' is and understanding what will be needed to achieve our goal. That is a tall order to expect of primary-aged children!

Whatever activities your child is doing, help them to appreciate the skills they are developing through it and explain how those skills can be improved and transferred to different situations.

Where can I find Gail?

Website: www.lessonsalive.com

Mailing list: https://bit.ly/tipsfromLessonsAlive

Instagram: @lessonsalive_gail_hugman

Facebook: @lessons Alive

Have you read my book *100 Things to Learn Before You're 10?*

Guiding your child as they learn and grow in this chaotic world, is an awesome responsibility and I know you want to do a good job.

This book draws on over 40 years teaching experience and can show you how to *make sure* your child understands their purpose, is motivated in their learning and keen to excel in life to the best of their ability.

Readers' comments:
'The book gets to the heart of the difference between wanting children to just DO something, and actually working with the children to want to do things for themselves, from homework to eating their supper and this is a really useful approach.'

'This book can be a **life-changer for many parents** (and their children). I find the brief illustrative case studies very engaging and full of wise words.

Applies to older children too.'

From just £5.99.

A Short and Simple Book for the Why's

Why do we teach what we teach? What should we be teaching a developing child, about themselves and their future? Why do so many children disengage from school, lack confidence or have low self esteem?

A Short and Simple Book for the Why's puts in a nutshell the messages children need to hear and the tips, reasons and activities that are helpful in encouraging children's core development, causing them to excel in school and in life.

It's a useful reference for parents who want to protect their children's enthusiasm for learning.

Readers' comments:
'This book is a little gem. Thanks so much for sharing these amazing tips with us all...'

'Gail's insight has astounded me! There is so much in this book to help parents understand the way a child's mind works is just fantastic.'

From just £5.99.